LILIES ARE

Waiting

Old Fashioned Poems

MARY BOWYER

LILIES ARE WAITING
OLD FASHIONED POEMS

iUniverse books may be ordered through booksellers or by contacting:

iUniverse
1663 Liberty Drive
Bloomington, IN 47403
www.iuniverse.com
844-349-9409

ISBN: 978-1-6632-4200-6 (sc)
ISBN: 978-1-6632-4201-3 (e)

Print information available on the last page.

iUniverse rev. date: 06/30/2022

Lilies Are Waiting

Show me a sign

That beneath the snow

Lilies are waiting,

Poised to grow.

For the wind is chill

And the air is cold

And the icicles,

They chill my soul.

So show me a sign

That beneath the snow

Lilies are waiting,

Poised to grow.

Lime Green Sapling

Lime green sapling,

Dancing to the music

    of a soft summer breeze.

I car-sit

    and drink up the warm air,

        the young tree, and the aqua waters.

Lush green sapling

On a street-corner arbor,

Seeming to caress me.

She bends as if to

cool the world.

To give us all her love,

    To give us summer.

Lush green sapling

On a street-corner arbor.

    Awe.

Almost

The editor wrote that she liked the verse

But sent it back, it could be worse,

She could have said it was no good

And, very nicely, that I should

Devote myself to house and home

And never write another poem.

Instead she wrote that she perused it

And almost, very nearly, used it.

I love to write, I will forever,

And an "almost" surely beats a "never."

In a Little Yellow Boat

Gliding across the water

Swans content

You and I

In a little yellow boat.

The ripples seem to understand

The secrets of the universe

We ask, they answer with their blue

In a little yellow boat.

Trees line the banks

And listen

To the wisdom of the ages

That permeates us as we float

In a little yellow boat.

Seasons

Flakes are falling, slow, haphazard.

Bitter wind, it stings my face.

Scarves and gloves and hats are pulled close

I'm longing for a warmer place.

A place where gloves are put away,

Where boots are nonexistent,

Where tan replaces wind and ice

Where slush and snow are distant.

I dream about an ocean breeze

And leaves and tans and flowers

I'll bask in that far-distant land

Upon the sand for hours.

But in the meantime,

Pull my coat close

And count each winter day

'Till springtime lifts her lovely head

And winter goes away.

Mary Bowyer

And as spring gaily trips along

And warms my hands and toes

I'll dream of Christmas songs and skis

And hope that soon it snows!

Magic Day

Blanket-sitting,

       surrounded

   by warm, white sand

      that kisses the peaceful blue

      of the lake.

My love and I watch

    as two little baby boys

Play catch, in the water,

    with inflatable dolphins.

My childhood rushes

    back to me

Like the flash of a movie scene.

Peace.

My Cat

I love my cat with love unbounded

So the very first time, I was simply astounded

After all, with all that petting

How could she lower herself to bed-wetting?

A cat so nice, a cat so sweet

But I went off and washed the sheet.

And then with evident delight

She did it again the very next night.

Now I'm washing sheets twelve hours a day

But telling it truly, I just have to say

That it really isn't such a quand'ry

(For I'm training her to do the laundry!)

Gray-Green Waves

Gray-Green waves

      Growing tides

To the shoreline

Ripples glide.

With my true love by my side

I watch white crests.

Love.

Bahai Temple

White cement pillars

Reaching, stretching, skyward

Lacey latticework, made for worship

I gaze, in awe.

White Crests

White crests rushing to shore

As if to tell a story

About vastness, perhaps

Or places only they have known

Or fish friends they have met

  And given a home.

The Blank Page

The fresh, blank page invites me,

Hugs, kisses, and excites me

And says, please fill me with your ink

And write, express, pause and think.

The fresh, blank page invites me,

Hugs, kisses, and excites me.

Deep, Inviting River

Deep, inviting river,

I have watched you many times

      but you never looked as beautiful

      as today,

      adorned in your finest blue,

We watch you, my love and I,

And drift and dream.

Beginnings

A gemstone,

Bright as a deep red sun,

Surrounded by small, sparkling rays.

You gave me this little ring

And, yes you gave me my first spring!

Kitchen

I like to knit in my living room

And there to music, listen.

But for a friendly evening chat

There's no room like the kitchen.

I like to, in the bedroom, read,

The front room dance and twitch in.

But for a talk with those I love,

There's no place like the kitchen.

At the Beach

Soft rolling waves kissing white sand,

Turquoise and aqua water,

A little dog jumps,

Against his friend bumps,

Like any self-respectful pup ought-a.

We sit on a bench,

My true love and I,

And take in the beauty, in awe.

And as they depart,

The owner and dog,

The little one holds out her paw.

Bird Song

The other day

    my tears flowed like rain

        As I sat alone in my car

           waiting.

    And then from the tree

        Opposite me,

    Green branches with love outstretched,

    Came a joyous song

The heartfelt chirp

      of a bird

        serenading...

And I knew somewhere deep down

    that that bird was my friend

        that he knew I was listening

           and sang to cheer me.

He sang like one ecstatic,

      chirrup, chirrup, chirrup

and each deep-throated note

    lifted my spirits

      a little bit more.

Thank you, little friend...

Springtime

The Springtime reaches out for me,

(I am in Winter's grasp,)

To rescue me from cold and chill,

To hear my shiv'ring gasp.

Her sunshine peeks through cloudy skies

To warm my waning spirit,

Her birdsong holds out promise warm,

It lifts my soul to hear it.

And when she finally frees me,

A song of songs I'll sing

And lift my glass and plant a flower

To toast my friend, the Spring.

Geneva

Driving around

This quaint little town,

Its old-fashioned shops,

Antiques, chocolate-fudge,

Give nostalgia a nudge.

The ambiance there

Takes me back to a Time

That I lived in a book

By Dickens,

sublime.

Driving around this quaint,

Little town

with you.

 Ball of Love

Warm, white furry ball of love

Was sent to me from God above.

To snuggle on cold nights so near

And purr sweet nothings in my ear.

Big, green loving eyes so sweet

Of hearing keen, of limb so fleet.

She gives my hand a lick, quite light

Her kitten way to say good night.

White Gleaming Snow

Soft white gleaming snow

Overlooking river's edge.

Children sledding down the hill,

Their grinning faces all aglow.

The piled-up snowflakes

Seem to hug,

And sing a song to me.

Winter beauty all around,

As far as I can see.

Miracle.

Love and Kisses

I love my guy

Like apple pie,

Like forests love the rain.

I'll kiss him once

And kiss him twice,

Then kiss him once again.

I love my guy

Like clear blue sky,

Like dewdrops love the flowers

I love him like a sunny day

Like flowers love the showers.

A Spring-like Sprout

A brand-new springlike sprout

I feel my roots

In the green.

Carrots, Pumpkins, Ripe Tomatoes

Carrots, pumpkins, ripe tomatoes

Dance upon their stalks,

And they please the bees and squirrels

And the birdie as she squawks.

Yes, I want to plant a garden,

Soft soil beneath my hands.

A special, lovely, garden,

And feel one with all the land.

Blues

I'm as down as down can be

Gray skies far as I can see

As if a wall surrounded me

As if the earth could yield no tree.

But usually my blues don't last

In minutes they are gone and past

So I know joy will soon be mine

And in my heart, the sun will shine.

Snowman

Want to build a band-new snowman?

We'll roll those snowballs till they're huge

And for his nose we'll place a twig.

When you see him, such surprise,

A smile that grins right to his eyes,

Those eyes made up of chunks of coal

That fill your heart and warm your soul.

You'll dance in sparkling, virgin snow

With a snow-clad world that smiles "hello."

I Long to Sew

I long to sew,

To pin a pattern

Yes, I know

I'll cut out pieces,

Darts and such

With a gentle touch

And all the joy my sewing brings

Oh yes, indeed

How my heart sings!

Magic.

Two-step

Nineteen hundred ninety-two

Have we, to our own selves, been true?

How much, of late, have we progressed?

Do we so modern, stand the test

Of time? It's true, we have surpassed

Undreamed-of dreams of time long passed,

We've sent a rocket to the moon,

Machines that think will be here soon,

The chains of slavery are gone,

For women's rights, a brand new dawn,

We've probed and analyzed the mind,

The brain, the thoughts of humankind,

But what about the surge in crime

And schools that get much worse as time

Goes by? And our polluted earth,

And of great leaders such a dearth?

I guess we've two-stepped on a track

Of one step forward, one step back

We must, now, giant footsteps take,

For our planet and our children's sake.

The Avenue

The avenue is wide,

Bright, even though

The day hides behind a cloud.

Folks don't stroll the avenue

They stride, with purpose

Their steps long and sure.

The avenue houses a music school.

Occasionally, a bass passes by,

Carrying its owner,

Sporting a stylish leather case,

Proudly.

Soft, sweet, sapling

Soft, sweet, sapling,

Swaying to and fro,

Struggling to touch the sky

As the summer breezes blow.

Soft, inviting, sapling,

She is a friend of mine.

Only angels from above

Can sculpt a life so fine.

Soft, sweet, sapling,

Swaying to and fro,

Struggling to touch the sky

As summer breezes blow.

My Screened-in Porch

Cornflower blue awning

Kisses white cotton-candy clouds.

I lie in my screened-in porch

You relaxing at my feet

And I am ecstatic.

Cornflower blue awning

Kisses white cotton-candy clouds.

Peace.

To My Son

Tomorrow you're coming home,

Just cannot wait.

I see your face spying us,

Last time we met.

The day, it was sunny

Sun shone down on you,

I felt oh so happy,

The sky, perfect-blue.

We'll drive to a restaurant

You, Daddy, and I,

Until tomorrow,

Let the time fly.

Your Warm, Loving Sunlight

I love you, dear lord

Take away my sharp sword

Move my body toward

Your warm, loving sunlight.

I love you dear God,

Tread on holy sod

Whenever you're near to me,

Thank you.

From Bookstore Perch

I window-gaze

From bookstore perch,

At daffodils

      of yellow hue.

Like sunshine, dancing

On the grass

I see them near

(One happy lass.)

I window-gaze

From bookstore perch,

At daffodils

And skies of blue.

To John Callaway

It's not because you're well-known, or because you're on TV

That I like you. Some famous folks I just don't care to see.

Nor is it 'cause your interviews expand my very being,

Excite my mind, engulf my heart – I'm as a blind man seeing.

No, it's more because behind those bright blue eyes of yours somewhere,

I sense a warm, kind, loving being, one who really cares.

In part, because I love to see the interview, the art

Of asking questions from the soul, of listening with the heart.

And if I were to write that someday novel I long to write,

And you were to me interview, to on your show invite,

And ask me who my heroes were, I'd simply have to say,

My heroes? I have just a few, and one's John Callaway.

Rolling ripples

Rolling ripples

Floating shore-ward

My love and I sit on our bench

Watching the wise and rambling river

We are all as one.

Geese and Popcorn

Rippling blue river

      Lightening my heart.

We watch geese together

As their curly necks bend,

As they scramble for food,

Some popcorn we send,

      To cheer their day.

Messy Living Room

I sit in messy living room,

I need a dustpan and a broom.

The clutter is 'bout six feet deep,

It seems to beg me, "sweep girl, sweep."

It seems to say, "No, do not wait,

Either way, you'll be up late..."

So I accede, I take the lead,

Tonight I'll simply plant the seed.

Little Pizza Shop

A little pizza shop,

Red-white tile décor

A comfy, home-y place,

I could not ask for more.

I love to sit, eat baklava,

My true love at my side,

Do crafting, reading, writing,

My smile is ten miles wide.

A little pizza shop,

Red-white tile décor

A comfy, home-y place,

I could not ask for more.

 Snowfall

The first real snowfall of the year

Flakes like glittering dust

Come dancing down and jump

      about

By winter winds are tossed

The drive is long

We lose our way

The snow obliterates the road

My heart is light

Like the feathery white

      of Winter

At the River

Blue, sparkling-diamond pond.

My love and I watch

The dancing ripples,

The sunlight

Doing handsprings

On the water.

Ecstasy.

Oh, So Hungry

I'm oh, so hungry,

Long for food,

Any kind that tastes real good.

Pizza, Chinese, Indian,

I'll eat it all, begin again.

(That way it will not go to waste

And I will know delicious taste.)

Sheldon Reuben

He wears a big and friendly grin,

The nicest man I know.

He's very simple, doesn't boast,

Or dress in fancy clothes.

He doesn't have expensive tastes

Or costly cars to drive.

But when he winks and smiles my way,

I'm so glad to be alive.

Lake Shore Drive

Crosstown highway

Bordered by an aqua lake.

We drive, my love and I,

Let out contented sighs.

I've never seen a city

So very, very, pretty.

I love Chicago.

Balloons

When I was a child,

I loved balloons.

Once I saw a movie

Which ended with

Hundreds of balloons

Floating high, high

Above a city,

Being set free.

They were alive to me,

Yes I was set free, too.

Seeing those balloons flying to heaven

To fly, to soar

To a magic place

Which I hope never

To leave completely.

After Weeks of Winter Gray

After weeks of winter gray,

Sun peeps out, I have to say,

Such joy comes to my weary heart,

Of all things warm I am a part.

After weeks of winter gray

It's such a magic, magic day.

Robins

Robins gliding,

Soaring southward

Not one goes his way alone

Seeming one with

Sky of sunshine

Sweet and graceful

Flying home.

A Snowy Day

I window-gaze

As snowflakes fall

I do not mind the snow at all,

The bushes cloaked in blankets white

A peaceful and inspiring sight.

As sparrows take to joyous flight.

I window-gaze

As snowflakes fall

I do not mind the snow at all.

A Little Library

Sitting in a little library,

The sun does handsprings

On the royal-blue carpet.

The walls are lined with book-friends.

I long to hug the tomes

That ask nothing in return

But to be read.

Soft, Blue Snow

Soft, blue snow

Covering green

Sight to be seen,

I linger and watch.

The park 'cross the street

Seems to reach out and hug me,

To tug me into

The soft blue snow.

The Swaying Dance of Flowers

I can't wait until flowers bloom,

Seen from my homey living room.

Daffodils and lilacs, too,

A season fresh and so brand new.

Buds and birth, a new beginning,

Inside, out, my head is spinning.

I could sit and watch for hours

The swaying dance of loving flowers.

Geese A' Waddling

The geese a'waddling through the grass

We stop the car to let them pass

And go upon their merry way

And leave us with such joy today.

Back to College

I long to go to college

To get an ed-ication.

To learn of things both large and small,

I'd feel such jubilation.

Economics, Social Science

Art and sculpture, math

I'd study hard

And get the most

From each and every clath.

Picking up where I left off,

Being filled with knowledge.

Although I'm sixty, I can't wait,

To go right back to college.

Spring's First Temporal Birth

The blossoms are bathed in golden sunlight

A magical aura of green.

Spring's first temporal birth

Later

      to give way to stronger

            longer-lasting leaves.

But, oh, her first children!

Lime and cloud-fluffy, delicate and dancing in the balmy breezes

As if to shout, "I have been born ---- dance with me."

Yes, I will dance with you --- you lovely babes whose days pass so quickly.

We will dance a dance of love and explode with joy in the dancing

And when you give way to your summer brothers

You will live on in precious memory.

What I Would Call a Writer

I don't want to waste a page

To say what I don't feel.

I want to love, express, create,

To put down what is real.

And in the putting down I want

To really feel the feeling.

To glance upon the written page,

See it my soul revealing.

Perhaps if I demanded less

My burden would be lighter.

But that would mean I'd never be

What I would call a writer.

When We Lie on the Grass

When we lie on the grass in the park

And your eyes gaze with love into mine

So limpid – so full of the nature around us

I dust off your nose with a blade of grass,

Then I know

That all of life's more unkind moments

Had their purpose in leading to

This one

Where I find my soul.

Through a Bookstore Window

Looking through a bookstore window

As the soft white feathers

Gently spread their winter joy.

Piling up in drifts of snow,

Fluffy whipped cream.

    Bringing love.

At the River

Blue, sparkling-diamond pond.

My love and I watch

The dancing ripples,

The sunlight

Doing handsprings

On the water.

Ecstasy.

Antique Shop

Pink teacups, molded china, dressed in garlands

Of blue and white flowers

So delicate, so very small.

A rocking-horse

Red-painted mane,

He really rocks,

So very tall,

With big brown eyes that seem to see.

I love to browse among the things

Some dusty, old

Belonging to

Another time

Yet seeming so at home in ours.

The lady of the shop is old, too.

Like her treasures on display,

With small blue eyes that twinkle bright

And long white hair like Queen Anne's lace.

And tales that cheer me through the night.

Children's Bookstore

Healthy, healthy,

Emotionally healthy.

Wealthy, wealthy,

So spiritually wealthy.

Everything seems right today.

The children's bookstore seems to say,

"Hello, hello," - A lovely day.

A Carpet of White

A carpet of white

      seems to invite

            lingering…

The little white hill

      I sit there, the snow,

            fingering

It is a wondrous, magic place

That in my soul,

      I do embrace,

A carpet of white

      seems to invite

            lingering...

White-Diamond Magic

White sparkle-drops drifting

We drive through the vanilla-ice-cream-covered streets

As the comforting flakes

Lift our spirits.

Chanukah.

Longing for Christmas

Longing for Christmas

For white-glistening snow

For red and blue lights

That dance, yes, and glow.

For snowmen with carrots

And children excited

And hot steamy tea

With all folks invited,

With strangers all smiling

and greeting each other

Friends giving a hug

And a laugh to each other.

Longing for Christmas

For white-glistening snow

For bright red and blue lights

That dance, yes, and glow.

Printed in the USA
CPSIA information can be obtained
at www.ICGtesting.com
CBHW070842260224
4674CB00011B/95

9 781663 242006